UNIVERSITY OF ULSTER LIBRARY

KW-223-694

WITHDRAWN
FROM THE LIBRARY OF
UNIVERSITY OF ULSTER

Benchmarking community participation

100476918

Benchmarking community participation

Developing and implementing the Active Partners benchmarks

Mandy Wilson and Pete Wilde

The **Joseph Rowntree Foundation** has supported this project as part of its programme of research and innovative development projects, which it hopes will be of value to policy makers, practitioners and service users. The facts presented and views expressed in this report are, however, those of the authors and not necessarily those of the Foundation.

Joseph Rowntree Foundation
The Homestead
40 Water End
York YO30 6WP
Website: www. jrf.org.uk

Mandy Wilson and Pete Wilde are Director Consultants with COGS Ltd. COGS is a consultancy organisation with extensive experience in the field of community development and specialises in community participation, strategic planning, partnership development and community-based research and evaluation.

© COGS 2003

First published 2003 by the Joseph Rowntree Foundation

All rights reserved. Reproduction of this report by photocopying or electronic means for non-commercial purposes is permitted. Otherwise, no part of this report may be reproduced, adapted, stored in a retrieval system or transmitted by any means, electronic, mechanical, photocopying, or otherwise without the prior written permission of the Joseph Rowntree Foundation.

A CIP catalogue record for this report is available from the British Library.

ISBN 1 85935 101 8   (paperback)
ISBN 1 85935 102 6   (pdf: available at www.jrf.org.uk)

Cover design by Adkins Design

Prepared and printed by:
York Publishing Services Ltd
64 Hallfield Road
Layerthorpe
York YO31 7ZQ
Tel: 01904 430033; Fax: 01904 430868; Website: www.yps-publishing.co.uk

Further copies of this report, or any other JRF publication, can be obtained either from the JRF website (www.jrf.org.uk/bookshop/) or from our distributor, York Publishing Services Ltd, at the above address.

Contents

100476918
PAW
307
1416
WIL

Foreword

This report chronicles one of the first initiatives taken up by Yorkshire Forward following the formation of the Board in December 1998. It was a time of energy and excitement. We were bringing together for the first time key economic and social agencies and were soon to forge the region's first economic strategy. We had only a skeleton staff – but that was part of the pioneering feel of the time.

The Churches Regional Commission (CRC) was also new on the scene. Colleagues on the CRC had taken an early interest in social inclusion and the future of the region's £750 million Single Regeneration Budget that would come under the remit of the Regional Development Agency (RDA). I had presented a paper entitled 'Community cohesion and capacity building' to the then Regional Chamber in November. It was from that piece of work that colleagues in the churches developed a simple and clear proposition. Community participation is key to regeneration, but is only patchily in evidence and we need benchmarks to measure it if it is to become general practice.

I took the proposal to the newly appointed Chief Executive of Yorkshire Forward, Martin Havenhand, in January 1999. The rest, as they say, is history. I am delighted that the Joseph Rowntree Foundation has sponsored this study of the development and application of Active Partners. Too often, funding bodies move from one initiative to another without learning the lessons from previous efforts. This study is a welcome corrective and makes a helpful contribution to good practice in community development.

The real heroes of the story are the men and women throughout the region who provide leadership in their communities. We should not be sentimental about participation. It is a hard task and increasingly unfashionable. We should not expect poor people to have a regard for their neighbours that richer people do not share. But the fact is that healthy communities depend on people knowing each other, acting together and forming a vision for the place they live in. Those who fund regeneration programmes need to build their work on this simple fact.

Benchmarks are always liable to misuse and misinterpretation. Quality is not identical to ISO9001 and community participation is not identical to Active Partners. But benchmarks make a difference. They encourage good practice, affirm those who do well and cajole those who could do better. The public have a right to know that their money is being used well. Those of us who argue for community-based regeneration have a duty as well as a need to measure and demonstrate that what we do has the effects that we claim for it. As Chair of the People Committee of the Yorkshire Forward Board until December 2002, I was in no doubt that clear measures strengthened my hand in arguing for investment in communities against other pressing calls on our budget.

I hope that the new Active Partners Unit will keep firm to this original vision. Regeneration in Yorkshire and the Humber has benefited, and will benefit, from the pioneering work that this study chronicles.

The Revd Dr Julian Cummins, Chair Churches Regional Commission for Yorkshire and the Humber, and Board Member Yorkshire Forward 1998–2002

Acknowledgements

We would like to thank and acknowledge the many individuals and organisations who have contributed to the development of Active Partners described in this report and in particular the following:

- The Churches Regional Commission for Yorkshire and the Humber who put forward the idea for the development of a benchmarking system.

- Yorkshire Forward RDA who have both funded and supported the work from its inception.

- The Regional Steering and Reference Groups that have guided the work throughout the process, principally:

Hilary Wilmer	Leeds Church Institute
Rosemary Suttill, Helen Thomson	Yorkshire and Humber Regional Forum for Voluntary and Community Organisations
Phil Back, George Baker	Humber and Wolds RCC
Shirley Hesselton	Staithes and Cowbar Residents' Association
Diane Shepherd	Sharrow Community Forum (formerly Manor and Castle Development Trust)
Claude Wray	Black Communities Forum
Deirdre Quill	Children's Society
Jim Brockbank, Ian Collins, Alan Matthews, Jill Duffy, Dee Meeneghan	Yorkshire Forward
Carol Cooper Smith, Margaret Jackson	Government Office for Yorkshire and the Humber
Peter Marcus	Joseph Rowntree Foundation.

- The Joseph Rowntree Foundation who part-funded and supported the final stages of the development project as well as the subsequent piloting and strategic development stages.

- COGS staff and associates who have been involved at different stages of development including Rose Ardron, Helen Bovey, Kate Jacob, Annie Rosewarne and Steve Rumbol.

- The many community members and representatives of regeneration partnerships and schemes who have contributed to the development of Active Partners, participating in workshops and conferences, responding to questionnaires and surveys, etc.

- And, finally, as Active Partners moves beyond our own remit, we acknowledge and welcome the work of the new Management Group and staff of the Active Partners Unit.

1 Introduction

For several years, community involvement has been promoted as being at the heart of government policy and programmes have been evaluated on that basis. 'Community capacity building', 'social capital', 'self-help', 'community control', 'resident-led', etc. are all terms that have become everyday language in both town hall corridors and active communities. Yet, studies have consistently shown that lip service has been paid to true community participation and that, in practice, public participation policy has often been found to be little more than rhetoric.

This report charts the development and implementation of a benchmarking framework designed to assist in the planning, support, assessment and evaluation of community participation in regeneration. This benchmarking framework is now commonly known as Active Partners following publication of the report *Active Partners – Benchmarking Community Participation in Regeneration* (Yorkshire Forward, 2000) in which the benchmarks are set out and explained.

Active Partners was initially developed for Yorkshire Forward, the Regional Development Agency (RDA) for Yorkshire and the Humber, in order to provide a set of benchmarks and measures to enable Single Regeneration Budget (SRB) schemes in the region to plan strategically and assess their performance in relation to community participation. It has since been perceived to have much wider application. Yorkshire Forward itself publicised and promoted Active Partners, both within the region and beyond, and the benchmarks have been taken up and used, in their original or adapted form, in an increasing range of contexts. Following a pilot project, Yorkshire Forward has developed an Active Partners forward implementation strategy. This has included the commissioning and establishment of an Active Partners Unit operating as part of the Yorkshire and Humber Regional Forum for Voluntary and Community Organisations.

We, the authors of this report, are community development consultants (COGS Ltd) who have been involved in work around the benchmarks over a three-year period. The purpose of this report is to share the process of developing and implementing Active Partners and some of the resulting outcomes and learning. Our research at the start of this development highlighted the scarcity of similar initiatives by other RDAs. We hope that this report will provide a useful resource for them and others in developing effective mechanisms to both support and assess community participation in regeneration. The work described provides a rare opportunity, certainly for us as consultants, to follow an idea from initial concept, through piloting, to mainstream practice.

The story begins with the development phase of Active Partners (1999–2000), follows its initial implementation (2000–01) and records its progress to date (October 2002).

2 Development

Beginnings

In the mid-1990s, the social inclusion sub-group of the Churches Regional Commission in Yorkshire and the Humber began to air its concerns about whether, and to what extent, community participation was actually happening in practice. The group reported anecdotal evidence of regeneration partnership lead bodies holding on to power despite the spirit of community participation inherent in the programmes they sought to implement. Three key points were highlighted:

1   that consultation processes were simply used as a stamp of agreement for plans already made

2   that there was a lack of participation in decision-making structures

3   that communities lacked control over resources.

In 1998, the Commission approached Yorkshire Forward and, in association with other voluntary and community organisations in the region, proposed that research was carried out to ascertain how best to achieve true community participation in regeneration.

Yorkshire Forward agreed to fund research, to be carried out under the lead of the Commission, the Regional Forum and other interested organisations in the voluntary and community sector (which became the Steering Group). COGS was commissioned to carry out the research, under the guidance of this Steering Group and this research developed into the benchmarks.

Yorkshire Forward, in agreement with the Steering Group, was united in the intention:

To deliver a clear benchmarking system for measuring the effectiveness of community involvement in social and economic regenerative activity in urban and rural areas. (Yorkshire Forward tender document 1999)

The process of development

The development of the benchmarks was carried out through an action research process intended to reflect the very spirit of community participation that the benchmarks would assess. The process aimed to:

* exemplify social inclusion throughout the process by actively engaging local people in establishing meaningful benchmarks

* underpin the work by research to establish good practice in community involvement both regionally and nationally

* include a methodology that would enable Yorkshire Forward to evaluate the development of community involvement in the region against agreed benchmarks

* ensure a reliable, robust and measurable process – capable of being applied to the full range of social inclusion initiatives.

Key features of the approach

The starting point for the action research was a recognition of the heterogeneity and elaborate nature of communities and the need for qualitative analysis that measures progress from diverse perspectives. Community participation was viewed both as a process and as an outcome and therefore the development of appropriate benchmarks was seen to require an understanding and prioritising of processes as well as indicating successful outcomes.

There were certain 'givens' (well researched starting points) in the development of the benchmarks:

* the need to understand communities – their composition, needs, priorities, tensions, strengths, existing networks, etc.

* the need for partnership working and resourcing of participation at all stages of the regeneration process and the need for recognition of long-term involvement

- the need for sensitivity around accountability and representation structures – building effective groups/structures that strengthen communities rather than divide them

- the need for a wider range of (formal and informal) ways in which people can participate – creating some community ownership and control

- the need for clarity and recognition of influence; for example, evidence that communities have been heard and that decisions have been informed by communities

- the recognition that people participate from a variety of starting points and cultural experiences and that this has implications for how people learn and contribute.

Involving all partners

The eight-month development process primarily involved people living in regeneration communities across the region but also local policy makers and officers charged with implementing SRB schemes, as well as academics and practitioners with relevant experience from outside the region. The emphasis on communities shaping the benchmarks was intentional, as their experience was crucial. But it was also recognised that the benchmarks had to reflect the lessons of research being carried out at the time and that they had to carry some meaning for those people in lead bodies who were likely to be responsible for applying them.

The process of developing the benchmarks was therefore fourfold:

1 a literature review of papers and publications

2 a series of workshops and meetings with people active at community level to help develop draft benchmarks and indicators

3 piloting of the materials with those people working to support partnerships and the implementation of regeneration programmes

4 a review of the draft materials by relevant academic and practice researchers.

Literature review

Thanks in part to the Internet, there was no shortage of research information. After trawling through scores of reports and books, however, we found little evidence of good practice or of approaches to assessing community participation in a regeneration context. In fact, this research illustrated that the same questions about community involvement and partnership working were being asked up and down the country. These questions provided a useful starting point for framing the development of benchmarks and a summary of them is included in Appendix 1.

Initially, the approach to benchmarking community participation was informed by the framework developed and promoted by the Scottish Community Development Centre – 'Achieving Better Community Development (ABCD)'. Its central focus is the identification of four dimensions of community empowerment that can be understood as both processes and outcomes. One of the starting points for consultations was to locate community participation and regeneration within this framework.

Community consultation

Four areas in the region were chosen, to reflect a range of communities, as the focus for community consultation and involvement in developing the benchmarks:

1 coalfield communities (Wakefield District and Dearne Valley)

2 a coastal zone (Bridlington, Scarborough and Hornsea)

3   inner-city and multi-racial communities (Sheffield and Rotherham)

4   rural communities (North Richmondshire).

In each of these areas, we invited community members who were active or interested in regeneration to participate in two workshops. Around 120 people were involved in total.

At the first workshop, participants worked through a series of participatory exercises to explore:

- key issues related to the local context

- what is required to support community empowerment

- enablers and barriers to community participation

- objectives for inclusion in community participation strategies.

An illustration of the workshop process: first development workshops

1   Participants were asked to identify something positive about their participation in regeneration; one less positive thing; and, crucially, one thing that would make a difference.

2   Participants shared the specific context in which regeneration was happening in their area – context statements were stuck onto 'clouds' all around the room.

3   Flip charts were provided for participants to record examples of what they felt was important and what they wanted to see in relation to the four ABCD dimensions of community empowerment. These were placed under the 'clouds' as a display wall:

(Continued)

- *Personal development and learning*: for example, what resources and opportunities are provided to enable local people to develop knowledge and skills?
- *Community equality*: for example, what is being done to identify and involve marginalised groups?
- *Community organisation*: for example, how is the effective development of new and established community groups and networks being supported?
- *Community influence*: for example, what resources, processes, structures, etc. are required to enable effective community participation and accountability?

4   Long strips of paper, each with a different title, were laid out on the floor leading to the display wall:
   - Pre-bid stage.
   - Scheme/partnership level – strategy.
   - Project level– management and delivery.
   - Wider community/outreach level.

5   Participants noted the barriers to (on red Post-its) and enablers of (on green Post-its) community participation and stuck them onto the appropriate strip.
   - Groups of participants took one strip each and, considering resources, processes and achievements, agreed some community participation objectives that they wanted to see as requirements of regeneration schemes and projects.

The information that these workshop provided (see Appendix 2) formed the basis for the development of the draft benchmarks and indicators. At this point, it became apparent from the material generated that the most appropriate themes around which to focus when considering community participation in regeneration should be communication, capacity, inclusivity and influence rather than the ABCD community empowerment dimensions. This was discussed in the second workshop sessions at which participants had the opportunity to comment on, amend and add to the draft materials.

An illustration of the workshop process: second development workshops

- After testing out the relevance of the four themes of communication, capacity, inclusivity and influence, cards with ideas generated at the previous workshops were laid out on four tables. Participants worked in groups to prioritise the objectives, by turning over those they disagreed with. Those cards left facing upwards were therefore assumed to have collective agreement and, following discussion around the turned over cards, final decisions were made around proposed benchmarks.

- Participants were given the opportunity to reword any benchmark statements they felt lapsed into jargon or were unclear.

- Participants shared their experience of good practice and developed checklists for implementation, thus generating potential benchmark indicators.

These development workshops had a broader outcome than simply contributing to the formulation of the benchmarks. They also provided a very useful networking opportunity for local people and groups. A limited amount of funding was provided to each workshop group to enable such contacts to be sustained and developed.

The piloting process

Communities had been centrally involved in the development of the benchmarks but we also wanted to know how realistic they were and the practicalities of implementing them. Officers and members of 13 SRB partnerships volunteered to take part in a short piloting process. This culminated in a workshop at which they shared practical suggestions for recording materials, evidencing practice and so on.

Initial hopes and fears

In April 2000, Yorkshire Forward published the developed benchmarks under the title *Active Partners – Benchmarking Community Participation in Regeneration* (Yorkshire Forward, 2000). In the foreword to this report, Julian Cummins, Yorkshire Forward Board Member and Chair of the Social Inclusion Task Group states:

> *Active Partners offers twelve benchmarks for communities and public policy makers to assess the extent to which community participation is taking place. It offers a toolkit for analysing weaknesses, suggestions for best practice and a framework for improvement ... Active Partners will encourage the best to do better, and the worst to reach the standards that will bring success ... I am convinced it will make a major contribution to sustainable regeneration.*

Thus, Active Partners was launched with enthusiasm and a commitment from Yorkshire Forward that the benchmarks would be used to assess bids to the Yorkshire Forward Development Fund (including the Single Regeneration Budget). The RDA felt that the benchmarks would help to develop understanding of community participation by all partners and provide the basis for the development and review of more effective community participation strategies. The development and launch of the benchmarks also need to be seen in the context of the related activities, at that time, of the People Committee of Yorkshire Forward as part of the SRB 6 process. This included the establishment of a community panel, the involvement of partners in funding decisions and the drafting of government guidelines:

> *What I saw as chair of the People committee throughout the SRB 6 process was really innovative and most people felt that it was, in process terms, a great advance.*
> (Julian Cummins, comments sent by email to COGS, January 2003)

Community members who knew about the benchmarks also enthusiastically welcomed Active Partners as reflecting the key issues and areas of practice that needed to be addressed for communities to participate effectively in regeneration. At the same time, some community members were anxious that lead bodies could use the benchmarks as a tool with which to hold communities themselves responsible for community participation, potentially blaming them if regeneration schemes did not meet Yorkshire Forward's community participation requirements.

Yorkshire Forward was moving into uncharted water and there were fears about the consequences as well as optimism that community participation would be enhanced through the benchmarking process. During the development phase, there were several debates within the steering group about whether the RDA should take a carrot or stick approach. Should partnerships be encouraged to apply the benchmarks voluntarily and receive a 'pat on the head' for playing their part, or should there be a degree of compulsion with penalties enforced for non-compliant partnerships? In the end, Yorkshire Forward enforced the use of 'a benchmarking system' for Round 6 SRB schemes from April 2000 and for all SRB schemes from April 2001. This decision raised a fear among many of the lead bodies that the benchmarks would be used to

compare schemes. Despite Yorkshire Forward's insistence that this would not be the case, many people perceived this to be the start of 'community participation league tables'.

Active Partners in a nutshell

Active Partners provides a framework that can be used by regeneration partnerships to develop an understanding of community participation. It helps to focus attention on what is already in place and what still needs to be achieved to maximise community participation. The framework is based on four important themes (dimensions) of community participation:

1 influence
2 inclusivity
3 communication
4 capacity.

While these dimensions interrelate, all four require careful consideration in order to develop opportunities for meaningful community participation. They provide an agenda for discussion between all those involved in regeneration.

Each dimension is further broken down into a number of aims to provide 12 benchmarks in total. These benchmarks describe what partnerships should be working towards.

Key considerations

Suggested questions for discussion (called 'key considerations') are provided for each benchmark (see Appendix 3).

For example, for the benchmark 'There is meaningful community representation on all decision-making bodies', the key considerations are 'How are communities represented on decision-making groups?' and 'How are decision-making processes enabling communities to be heard and to influence?'

Figure 1 The four dimensions of community participation

Influence	Inclusivity
How partnerships involve communities in the 'shaping' of regeneration plans/activities and in all decision making.	How partnerships ensure all groups and interests in the community can participate, and the ways in which inequality is addressed.
Communication	**Capacity**
How partnerships develop effective ways of sharing information with communities and clear procedures that maximise community participation.	How partnerships provide the resources required by communities to participate and support both local people and those from partner agencies to develop their understanding, knowledge and skills.

Figure 2 The 12 benchmarks of community participation

Influence	Inclusivity
1 The community is recognised and valued as an equal partner at all stages of the process. 2 There is meaningful community representation on all decision-making bodies from initiation. 3 All community members have the opportunity to participate. 4 Communities have access to and control over resources. 5 Evaluation of regeneration partnerships incorporates a community agenda.	1 The diversity of local communities and interests is reflected at all levels of the regeneration process. 2 Equal opportunities policies are in place and implemented. 3 Unpaid workers/volunteer activists are valued.
Communication	**Capacity**
1 A two-way information strategy is developed and implemented. 2 Programme and project procedures are clear and accessible.	1 Communities are resourced to participate. 2 Understanding, knowledge and skills are developed to support partnership working.

The purpose of the key considerations is to help those using the benchmarks to relate them to their own practice. In answering these questions, partnerships can begin to identify their current position and possible future action. *Active Partners* (Yorkshire Forward, 2000) also contains suggestions and examples of practice for each of the benchmarks as well as a listing of possible indicators that could be used to measure and assess progress.

Underlying principles

The following guidance notes from the *Active Partners* report (Yorkshire Forward, 2000) summarise the underlying principles in applying the benchmarks.

- The benchmarks should inform the planning of regeneration schemes from the very start.

- They are applicable across the range of contexts, themes and starting points in which regeneration activities are taking place.

- They can help to raise the profile of community participation and its role within regeneration.

- They can initially be used to develop the understanding of community participation by all partners.

- They provide a framework for the development of clear and effective community participation strategies within which clear objectives and action plans are developed for progress in relation to each benchmark.

- The use of the benchmarks either for planning or review should not be a tick-box exercise but a process in which communities themselves participate.

- The benchmarks should be used to compare and share experience and achievements in order to support best practice. However, any use of the benchmarks for comparing progress across schemes has to take account of the different contexts and starting points within which they are operating.

- The benchmarks were developed within a regeneration context. However, the concept of community participation is relevant across many programmes and policies including health (Health Action Zones), children (Sure Start) and planning (Local Strategic Partnerships). The benchmarks are therefore applicable and adaptable to a variety of settings.

The process of benchmark application

To accompany the Active Partners framework and benchmarks, COGS subsequently produced a further set of guidelines for those applying the framework. These suggested a staged approach involving the following five key steps:

1 developing a shared understanding of community participation
2 establishing the current position
3 identifying issues and needs to be addressed
4 agreeing an action plan
5 reviewing progress.

Step 1: developing a shared understanding of community participation

Communities are made up of people with a variety of interests and identities. It is therefore important to share some understanding of:

- *the benefits of community participation – why it is important*

- *who the 'community' is – i.e. the different groups and interests that make up the community, such as distinct neighbourhoods, faith groups, women and men, disabled and non-disabled people, age groups, etc.*

- *the key dimensions of community participation – influence, inclusivity, communication and capacity, and what they mean to different people.*

Step 2: establishing the current position

A baseline position can be ascertained by identifying where your community is now in relation to the benchmarks. The key considerations attached to each benchmark should help you to focus on the significant questions. Taking each one in turn, you could look at what has been achieved – this is an opportunity to recognise and celebrate achievement as well as where you might be facing difficulties.

Step 3: identifying issues and needs to be addressed

Establishing the current position should help to highlight issues that need to be addressed. It is particularly important that you gather the views of the different interests represented within your community to ensure that all perspectives are shared. You can also begin to identify the different activities that will help to develop greater and more meaningful community participation.

Step 4: agreeing an action plan

Try to set yourselves a target for at least one benchmark from all four dimensions to ensure that there is a holistic approach to community participation. It is important to be realistic about what is achievable within any given timescale and the level of resources available. You will probably need to agree priorities and to identify other groups and agencies that will lend their support. You may find the examples of practice and the indicators of achievement that are outlined for each benchmark in Active Partners (Yorkshire Forward, 2000) act as useful 'prompts'.

Step 5: reviewing progress

Community participation strategies should be reviewed in the light of progress made and outstanding needs. This is not just about what processes and procedures are in place but how effective these are. For example, in relation to the benchmark 'There is meaningful community representation on all decision-making bodies', a review may involve an assessment of:

- *numbers of community members involved, the ratio of community representatives to other stakeholders on partnership boards and on other decision-making bodies/forums*

- *what has and what has not worked in terms of community influence, the extent to which different community interests and agendas have been reflected and represented in decision-making processes*

- *the degree to which a wide range of community groups 'feel' there is a democratic process.*

(COGS, 2001a)

3 Road testing the benchmarks

Beginnings

Although there was initially a positive response to the Active Partners benchmarks, it was also recognised that the real proof of the pudding would be in the eating. It was only when Active Partners was applied in practice that Yorkshire Forward, and all other stakeholders, would be able to assess the merits, or otherwise, of the benchmarking approach. With this in mind, the Joseph Rowntree Foundation (JRF) offered to match fund an action research project in the Yorkshire and Humber Region to road test the benchmarks and their application. This was one element of a JRF project through which complementary road testing of both Active Partners and another set of community participation audit tools developed for JRF by Danny Burns and Marilyn Taylor (2000) was to be carried out in different regions. Yorkshire Forward responded to the challenge and agreed to contribute to the financing of this road-testing project.

We, COGS, were commissioned a second time, this time by JRF. The project was to be developmental and to focus on:

- how well the benchmarks can assess the level and quality of community involvement in regeneration

- the impact of Active Partners on the sharing of good practice within and between partnerships

- how well Active Partners can encourage partnerships and other organisations to identify and remedy bad practice

- the extent to which Active Partners can encourage a culture change towards community participation in regeneration partnerships and in individual partner agencies

- ways in which the benchmarks and the process of assessment can be adapted and applied to different regeneration programmes and contexts.

Building on the initial Steering Group, a Regional Reference Group was established, representing the interests of the Churches Regional Commission, the voluntary and community sectors, Yorkshire Forward and Government Office for Yorkshire and the Humber.

The process of road testing

COGS supported the implementation of Active Partners and assessed the relevance and effectiveness of the benchmarks through an action-based research and capacity-building approach. This included:

1 Hosting conferences and a series of workshops around use of the benchmarks for regeneration schemes, community activists and RDA scheme managers including:
   - eight sub-regional workshops for SRB scheme representatives (totalling 130 participants)
   - four sub-regional workshops for community members (70 participants)
   - a workshop for Yorkshire Forward project managers
   - a region-wide conference for community members (70 participants)
   - a region-wide conference for people working closely with SRB and other regeneration programmes (85 participants).

2 Supporting selected SRB schemes to apply Active Partners in order that they might assess the level and quality of community participation including the provision of:
   - ongoing support to three contrasting 'case study' schemes from across the region
   - additional guidance notes both for schemes and for community members.

3 Collecting information about the range of ways in which Active Partners has been applied by partnerships, schemes and projects including:

- visiting a range of regeneration schemes and partnerships across the region (nine visited)
- carrying out two postal questionnaires to all schemes and some community members in the region
- carrying out telephone interviews with nine SRB schemes.

4 Facilitating the sharing of practice (good and bad) between partnerships and schemes, related both to the application of Active Partners and to the implementation of community participation strategies.

Examples of workshop exercises designed to help apply Active Partners

Who is our community and who should we try to involve?
- Place several pieces of flip-chart paper on the floor or on a table with a series of circles, each with a heading, e.g service users, minority ethnic communities, economic communities, community groups, locally managed voluntary groups, faith communities, age-based groups, geographical communities, communities of interest, communities of identity, workplace communities.

- Ask participants to identify all of the groups that fall into the circles, to write them onto cards and place them in the appropriate circle.

- Examine the picture created and facilitate a discussion about which groups are not currently involved and what can be done to improve participation from across the circles.

The 'map' of groups and communities can form a useful display to which individuals

(Continued)

and groups can add, if placed in public spaces.

What is our baseline position and what action can we take to increase participation? This exercise provides a good starting point for developing community participation strategies.

- Draw speedometers on to A3 sheets of paper with a benchmark statement underneath each one (see Figure 3). Place them on the wall or on tables, clustered around communication, capacity, inclusivity and influence.

- Ask participants to mark a line onto the speedometer at the point they think the project, scheme, programme in question has reached.

- Participants identify what has helped to get them to this 'speed' and/or action to help 'speed up'.

- The action points can then be prioritised, each with an agreed timescale and milestones that will indicate progress.

Implementation by lead bodies of schemes and partnerships

Applications

Yorkshire Forward had circulated copies of *Active Partners* (Yorkshire Forward, 2000) to all of the SRB partnerships in the region. Many officers from lead bodies were already aware of the benchmarks through their involvement in earlier consultations. Through the road-testing project, people working with SRB partnerships and schemes identified a range of development activities that Active Partners promoted and helped. Nine of these are summarised below; the quotes are all anonymised but all are from local authority and SRB scheme officers.

Figure 3 An example of the speedometer used in the workshop exercise

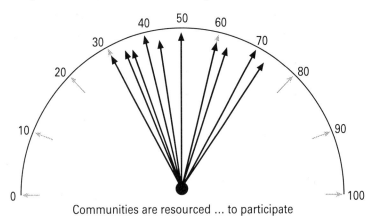

Communities are resourced ... to participate

Partnership development

The process of using Active Partners has helped to break down 'sectoral' myths, which in turn has enabled the development of 'true (better) partnerships':

> *A day was held for all agencies [private, public, voluntary] to understand Active Partners – this helped to break down barriers and improve understanding; it helps to raise people's awareness of the process of voluntary–community sector differences and how the statutory sector works.*

Strategic planning

Active Partners has helped to raise awareness of community participation and has been used as a guideline for developing community participation strategies:

> *It helps to focus on what we are trying to do, i.e. community participation – it's a resource for holding statutory agencies to account and is a power tool for communities to demand involvement; it also shows the Government our commitment to involving the community and shifting the balance of power.*

Assessment and measuring progress

Active Partners has been used both in developing funding bids and then evaluating levels of involvement in the funded scheme or project:

> *As a measuring tool for effective community participation and evaluating where we are at the moment – something to measure against; helps you to sit back and refocus.*

In Withernsea and Holderness, £7,000 was budgeted into the delivery plan for support and measurement including 'Active Partners compliance'.

Capacity building

Active Partners has provided a tool for public and private sector capacity building. Some people have used it as a resource for educating officers in statutory agencies; and, by promoting understanding and awareness of the community regeneration process, it has helped to identify training needs around community involvement. Some scheme officers saw it as an 'index' to community participation and, as one person commented, 'it helps people to realise what they don't know'. This understanding enabled some officers to recognise the complexity of community participation and to acknowledge that participation takes time to develop:

> *We now really see the value of a year zero from the community development perspective ... community participation needs to be built into schemes even before bids are compiled, as it should be integral to development.*

Forward strategy development

Active Partners can initiate evaluation and therefore promotes the development of successor structures as part of a sustainable forward strategy. In Dewsbury, where Active Partners was introduced towards the end of a scheme's life, the benchmarks have been effectively used as a framework for demonstrating what had been achieved in the area in order to (successfully) help access future funding. In Rotherham, COGS carried out part of the final evaluation of an SRB scheme using the Active Partners framework. The findings of this evaluation have informed the community participation strategy for a subsequent Neighbourhood Management programme in the same area.

Promoting community participation to others

The understanding that comes from working through the benchmarks helps to unpick the strands of what community participation means in practice. This makes it easier to articulate both the need for community participation and the areas of practice that need to be addressed in order to enhance participation:

> *Active Partners would be a useful outline for a training course for people from different council departments to help them to understand community participation.*

Making changes

Active Partners helps to question methods of working and the extent to which community participation really happens:

> *Active Partners facilitates the change process – helps to ring the alarm bell and unblock sticking points in the regeneration process – to force new ideas and provide an outline for action.*

> *More effective partnerships with the community have been built based on the 'key considerations' in Active Partners.*

> *It led to the creation of community reps on programme delivery groups.*

Linking the local with the strategic

Application of Active Partners at a local level can help to inform community participation processes within the development of wider strategic partnerships, for example, by making connections between SRB management boards and the Local Strategic Partnership:

> *… it can improve very local partnership working and encourage a bottom-up approach at the wider level.*

Designing new projects

Using Active Partners from the start in new programmes (e.g. Neighbourhood Management) can help to inform and shape the whole initiative:

> *We have learnt from this* [experience of applying Active Partners] *and are trying to ensure that the community structures that have been set up play an important role in developing new funding bids.*

Examples of benchmark application

- *Manor and Castle SRB 3 Scheme in Sheffield* carried out a baseline assessment of community participation using Active Partners. Three workshops were held to begin applying the benchmarks – a half-day staff training event, a half-day meeting of programme managers and a half-day exercise with the board. Each benchmark was reproduced onto an A3 sheet with examples of possible indicators and two boxes to write in 'what we are doing now' and 'what we could do'. People considered each benchmark in small groups and swapped them all round so everyone commented on all 12. Each group had slightly different perceptions and ideas for future action. The worker who facilitated the sessions then collated and wrote up everyone's comments to produce a report which for each benchmark included the baseline position, planned action and additional proposals. This has provided the basis for an action plan. The scheme is planning to invite community forums in the area to audit the progress made over the next year.

- *Withernsea SRB 2 Scheme* held a workshop for a variety of stakeholders including community members (including youth forum representatives), primary care group, youth service and SRB programme staff. In all, 36 people contributed to the process. A facilitator helped the group to examine the benchmarks and key considerations so they could produce locally relevant indicators. This allowed them to draw together information about the baseline position and to devise specific actions that would address their indicators and meet their high priority targets. This forms a draft action plan. The exercise enabled participants to identify significant issues and to share in quality discussions about them. A great deal was achieved in a relatively short but intensive amount of time.

- *Hull PACTS* is an example of how Active Partners can be applied to contexts other than SRB schemes. PACTS are local partnership boards developed to deliver Objective 2 funding. A workshop which involved about 25 people, the majority of whom were community members, was held for members of local PACT boards across Hull. A flip chart which listed the benchmarks and key considerations for each of the four Active Partner dimensions was provided. Individually or in pairs, participants thought about each dimension in relation to the role of the PACT boards. 'Post-its' were provided for people to record achievements, key concerns and requirements for effective community participation. There was then a sharing and discussion of the points raised in relation to each dimension. The end product was a set of draft benchmarks and key considerations specific to the role and work of the PACT boards.

Difficulties encountered

Although there was generally a positive approach to applying Active Partners, experience shows that it has not always been easy. A number of issues arose during the 'road-testing' process.

- Some partnerships saw Active Partners as yet another piece of bureaucracy from the RDA and felt that placing Active Partners alongside SRB bureaucratic processes was unhelpful:

  > ... [scheme] *officers can be seen as the foes of community organisations as they have to enforce these 'over the top' rules.*

- There was a questioning of the term 'benchmarks' – either because people felt that the statements of achievement were not directly quantifiable or because they felt the term did not sit comfortably with the process of participation.

- Officers committed to applying the benchmarks were frustrated that lip service was sometimes paid to community participation by some partners; and some found commitment from their own colleagues hard to come by:

  > ... *to implement Active Partners is hard because of the relative* [lack of] *power of the programme manager to other managers in the accountable body.*

- Fully implementing Active Partners and the development of a participation strategy was a lengthy process and some people commented that it was difficult to keep up the momentum.

- Officers sometimes struggled to effectively engage communities in working with them to implement Active Partners, especially where there were contextual difficulties, e.g. wide geographical area, diverse communities and overlapping regeneration boundaries.

- There were differences in knowledge and awareness around what working with communities really meant, as well as sometimes a basic lack of understanding by some of the personnel charged with implementing Active Partners.

- Some partnerships felt that the timing of the introduction of benchmarks was unhelpful. Some SRB Round 6 schemes argued that they were just getting off the ground and needed more time to sort out delivery plans first, while some of the earlier schemes said it was too late for them to take the benchmarks into account.

The findings of road-testing research illustrated that, while most officers responsible for applying the Active Partners framework were committed to the exercise, many lacked the skills and full understanding to develop simple but creative rather than bureaucratic processes, to usefully apply the framework to their own context and purpose. It would also be unwise to underestimate the antagonism to Active Partners shown by a significant minority. There was evidence of resistance in a few partnerships and some officers found it hard to comprehend that Active Partners might be relevant to their own structures.

Implementation by Yorkshire Forward

Yorkshire Forward, in its capacity as the funding delivery agency for SRB programmes, made its position on community participation very clear when it commissioned the development of the benchmarks and subsequently published *Active Partners* (Yorkshire Forward, 2000) and recommended its application by schemes. Guidelines were issued initially to all SRB Round 6 schemes and subsequently to all schemes from all SRB Rounds:

It is important that all Partnerships understand the importance and demonstrate a commitment to community participation in regeneration and to that end put in place systems and strategies to support and enhance participation and effectively monitor the level and quality ... It is recommended that the benchmarks set out in Active Partners be used ...

Partnerships should note that it is important to have community involvement in the assessment process itself and that all reports on progress should be made public.

(Yorkshire Forward Guidance Notes for Round 6 Partnership Delivery Plans, August 2000)

There were concerns, however, about the nature of Yorkshire Forward's commitment to the principles of Active Partners.

- Yorkshire Forward's Regional Economic Strategy, at that time, appeared to give little recognition of the relevance and importance of community participation to economic regeneration. There were criticisms, from local SRB scheme officers in particular, that community participation was not 'at the heart of Yorkshire Forward' and that partnerships were therefore being asked to do something that had no meaning.

- Identified barriers to community participation were sometimes seen to be outside the control of local partnerships and were sometimes created by requirements imposed by the RDA itself. This raised questions about how Yorkshire Forward used the benchmarks to assess its own practice and procedures, and its impact on local regeneration and community involvement:

They [Yorkshire Forward] *need to understand the impact of their role on community participation, e.g. how long it takes for things to happen and the knock-on effects of things like delays in getting delivery plans signed off.* (SRB scheme officer)

It is important that Yorkshire Forward gets across a positive message and gives clarity to its own role and obligations with regard to community participation. (SRB scheme officer)

- In the early stages of implementation there was some confusion about what was required:

  Yorkshire Forward imposed this without adequate guidance about reporting procedures. Every other area of their work has clear guidelines of what is to be provided to Yorkshire Forward, except this.
  (SRB scheme officer)

- Yorkshire Forward staff expressed a lack of clarity about their roles in relation to Active Partners and a lack of confidence to make judgements about what is, and what is not, effective community participation.

- There was some inconsistency in what people were being advised by Yorkshire Forward staff across the sub-regions. One SRB scheme officer reported being informed by a Yorkshire Forward officer that:

  SRB is not the right place for community participation – other schemes like New Deal for Communities had been set up to do this.

- Schemes and communities questioned how Yorkshire Forward evaluated and made use of the information it collected in relation to the benchmarks. Many people living in regeneration communities, as well as schemes that were conscientiously using Active Partners, believed that Yorkshire Forward needed to be more challenging:

  Active Partners was a prerequisite of funding for SRB 6 but the RDA does not seem to have the inclination or the teeth to clamp down on those not doing anything. (SRB scheme officer)

This concern, also voiced by members of the Active Partners Reference Group, highlighted the fact that Active Partners was so far failing to provide a mechanism for calling to account those partnerships and schemes that were not even beginning to effectively address issues related to community participation. It was clear that the benchmarks themselves could not fulfil this function unless they were more clearly linked both to explicit sanctions and to more effective and consistent reporting requirements and procedures.

Clearly, these were very real concerns but they should be seen in the context of the positive investment and commitment given by Yorkshire Forward to the development of the benchmarking process. Yorkshire Forward's approach to implementing the benchmarks is being increasingly accepted and embraced by SRB partnerships and many have valued the flexible approach taken by the RDA. Yorkshire Forward policy officers have welcomed the feedback provided through the road-testing project and have sought to address the issues raised through the development of the future implementation strategy.

Implementation in a wider context

The Local Government Act 2000 gives local authorities powers to support community participation – with an increasingly high profile given to community development as a means of building social capital. The road testing showed that Active Partners could make a valuable contribution to assessment processes developed as part of any new initiatives concerned with community participation. There was evidence, gathered through the project, that the benchmarks were being used outside SRB schemes (and outside the region) and that they were applicable to most projects and partnerships where there was a commitment to community participation; for example, in New Deal for Communities Programmes, Neighbourhood Management Pathfinders, Health Action Zones, European Objective 2 (Priority 3) funded projects and Market Towns Initiatives. It was also suggested that Active Partners was suited to other schemes where local control is a central design feature, for example,

Healthy Living Networks and Sure Start Schemes, and to the development of Local Strategic Partnerships.

Thus, many people believed that the Active Partners benchmarks deserved to be taken seriously by a broad range of organisations and that their application needed to be cross-cutting. This was reiterated by Yorkshire Forward staff who felt their job would be easier if the same guidelines were applied to other strategic partnerships. Following the government decision not to have any further rounds of the SRB programme and to give Government Offices responsibility for the Neighbourhood Renewal Fund, the position of the RDA in relation to regeneration funding was increasingly one of influence rather than decision making. The Government Office in the region, while unwilling to be prescriptive, has signposted partnerships to Active Partners and perceives it to be of benefit to the programmes and initiatives it oversees.

Active Partners has been used and adapted for a range of different purposes. There are examples of Active Partners being used as a development tool; for example, some community work teams have used Active Partners as a strategic checklist around community participation issues and community groups have used the benchmarks to assess their own performance. In addition, Active Partners has been used as the 'base model' or starting point for the development of several new frameworks including 'Well connected', a self-assessment tool initiated by Bradford Health Action Zone and Bradford Communities Partnership. 'Well connected' aims to assist organisations to evaluate their actions around community involvement through consideration of six headline themes and a self-assessment scoring process.

Community perspectives

Community activists, particularly those involved in the development of the benchmarks, demonstrated a great deal of continuing support for and commitment to the benchmarking process. They believed that it provided an important means of promoting and enhancing community participation:

> *Active Partners has a respected background which gives it legitimacy and a sense of ownership.*
> (Community workshop participant)

Active Partners has also encouraged some communities to challenge traditional consultation approaches and methods of community engagement, and to become more actively involved:

> *It's given the 'real' community some ammunition to challenge some of the restrictions placed upon it.*
> (Community member)

There were also examples of community representatives using Active Partners as a 'backing tool' to assert their views.

Examples, gathered through the road-testing project, of Active Partners making a positive contribution from the perspective of community members include the following.

- In Sheffield, the dimensions of community participation were used to provide workshop themes at a conference to develop an emerging new community partnership.

- In Hull, the 'inclusivity' dimension of Active Partners was used to help community members to consider the purpose and role of Community Panels.

- In Hornsea, where Active Partners is seen as providing guidelines for practice, it helped to move the regeneration process forward and to involve more people.

Some community groups and networks used Active Partners to consider their own role and practice in relation to community participation. For example, a Community Forum in Sheffield held a series of Active Partners workshops for local people, using the benchmarks to gather their views and ideas about opportunities for involvement in regeneration initiatives in the area. The outcomes of these workshops helped the Forum to review both its own processes and procedures for community participation and its role in facilitating involvement in local regeneration.

Illustration of process

- Several Active Partners sessions were held across the geographical area and with targeted groups of people – Community Forum trustees, women, children and young people.

- 'Speedometers' (see Figure 3 earlier in this report) were used to find out where people felt they were in relation to participation and what would help to increase participation.

- Children compiled their own 'regeneration dictionary', putting jargon into their own words.

- Young people role-played situations in which they felt they were listened to, and where they were not, and discussed what made a difference.

- A local map of the different types of community interest, community groups, agencies working in the area, networks and partnerships was created.

- A concluding workshop, at which children drew a picture of a child-friendly area and
  (Continued)

made proposals for their continued involvement, and adults developed objectives for future action, was held bringing together a whole range of interests.

Overall, the road-testing project found a much lower level of awareness of Active Partners among community members than among paid regeneration officers. It was also found that community members sometimes faced a brick wall when trying to use Active Partners to support change within their partnerships and schemes. They were often unable to make effective use of Yorkshire Forward when wanting to endorse or challenge the practice of partnerships and schemes because they had little knowledge of staff structures and personnel, or of decision-making processes, or of the relationship between the RDA and SRB schemes on the ground. Concern was also expressed by some communities that the benchmarks could be used 'against' communities themselves if lead bodies mistakenly used the benchmarks just to scrutinise the community itself rather than assessing either themselves or the partnership. These difficulties highlighted the need for more effort in promoting Active Partners within regeneration communities. The eight-page *Active Partners – Benchmarking Community Participation, Guidance Notes for Communities* (COGS, 2001b) has helped by providing a basic introduction to the benchmarks that is much easier to read than the original long report. Perhaps more importantly, the workshops and conferences targeted at community members from regeneration areas as part of our work around Active Partners provided, for many, the first opportunity to network across communities. This highlighted the need to further develop such networking events and to draw more communities into such opportunities.

The impact of Active Partners

Since Active Partners was first developed, major contextual changes have complicated an assessment of its impact. Numerous new initiatives that require and support community participation have been introduced. Running alongside this is the rapid development of measurement and indicator models. Many local authority officers in particular are expected to use a variety of models and tools to assess the same areas of work, especially where there are a number of different funding sources being used. Active Partners is likely to be just one of these. The extent, then, to which Active Partners alone has stimulated a difference in enhancing and improving 'real' participation is difficult to quantify, though we do have some evidence (outlined below) of the initial effects of its application.

In addition, it is still early days in the life of Active Partners and it has taken time to develop an implementation momentum and therefore to show real results in what is anyway the often slow process of engagement:

Community participation and capacity building pays dividends over time – it is a long-term investment, not a quick fix. (SRB scheme officer)

Schemes themselves are as heterogeneous as communities and, by Spring 2001, they were at very different stages and levels of commitment – from a reluctance to undertake a 'bureaucratic' requirement, to enthusiasm for having the opportunity and framework to address community participation in a more overarching way. At the end of the day, real impact will be measured by the extent of enhanced community participation brought about as a consequence of the benchmarking process.

Evidence from the road-testing process did, however, illustrate that the application of Active Partners was raising awareness of community participation, stimulating change and providing a framework for reviewing progress and practice. Benefits reported from the process of application included:

- the opportunity to reflect on successes and to review participation

- the confidence to back up ideas was provided by Active Partners

- raised awareness and highlighting of gaps to be addressed

- widened involvement and the development of a more inclusive community representation

- the potential to adapt the framework for each individual scheme

- the potential to use the framework and principles in other programmes and strategies, e.g. Sure Start, European funding programmes, community planning, etc.

Active Partners has already highlighted for many schemes and partnerships the resource implications of enabling effective community participation. There has been evidence of situations where the requirement to apply Active Partners has prompted partnerships either to set up dedicated working groups or to employ workers specifically to take a lead on work around community participation. For example, two regeneration schemes in Sheffield have recruited community participation workers with a remit to co-ordinate the development and implementation of community participation strategies for the schemes, in consultation with all stakeholders, including communities.

On a more negative note, experiences gathered in the road-testing project highlighted the continuing existence, in some instances, of many of the issues identified in the initial benchmarking research.

- Regeneration processes still felt very top down.

- Community activists felt their input and capacity to deliver projects was not recognised.

- Senior partners were often not prepared to devolve enough power and spend enough money to make participation work.

- Resourcing community participation was a big issue – there was a lack of support for communication between community groups and for passing information across communities.

- There was little consideration given within either regeneration programmes or the delivering bodies (funders and partnerships) to the knowledge and skills required to expand community involvement. There were also examples of the responsibility for community participation being passed to workers with no specific skills or understanding of this specialist area of work.

- There was a lack of clarity about who community representatives 'represented' and they were rarely given sufficient support, resources, or mechanisms to help them to feed back to their constituency. The community was also sometimes represented by 'hand-picked puppets' and voluntary sector selective gatekeepers.

- Equal opportunities policies were usually in place but there were few opportunities for training or support to put the policies into effective practice.

- There was a lack of information available in community languages and there were not enough black and minority ethnic workers employed on regeneration schemes.

There was also, as stated earlier in this report, little evidence of situations where the benchmarks were being used to 'call to account' and really challenge those partnerships and schemes that were felt to be both weak in terms of community

participation and unwilling to recognise this fact or do anything about it. We believe this is partly due to the apparent lack of coherence and rigour in Yorkshire Forward's own assessment procedures referred to earlier. It also highlights the need for clear processes and procedures through which community members themselves can endorse or challenge the community participation practice of regeneration activities operating in their communities. Some people active in their own regeneration communities have called for a regulatory body to scrutinise the role of key organisations in community participation.

The continuing requests for additional training and support around Active Partners alongside continuing concern that some partnerships and schemes were still 'getting away with' tokenism suggest that, while Active Partners had achieved a positive impact, there was a need for a bit more carrot and a bit more stick.

Lessons for future implementation

We analysed what seemed to be at the root of people's lack of understanding and/or use of Active Partners. It became apparent that, on the whole, SRB officers and board members were keen to develop community participation but were often struggling to begin – perhaps because this is a whole new approach to their work and they require further guidance and skilled facilitative support.

The schemes that appeared to have made most progress with Active Partners were those with dedicated community development staff (either as part of the programme administration or as separate projects). This highlights the fact that the Active Partners benchmarks are not enough in themselves to bring about change. What is also required is someone with an understanding of community participation and the skills to develop and facilitate processes through which the stakeholders in any regeneration activity can begin to relate the benchmarks to their own context and use them as a framework for dialogue and development.

Clarity of the benchmarks and understanding of Active Partners

There were some very mixed views about the 'accessibility' of the benchmarks. These ranged from 'they couldn't be any clearer' and 'comprehensive and self-explanatory' to 'they are too jargonistic'. Despite the broad community involvement in the initial design of the benchmarks, some people found the terminology off-putting. It is interesting to note, however, that those making the most vocal statements about style and language – for example, 'they are not accessible enough for the community' and 'people struggle with the underpinning intellectual concepts' – were often paid officers rather than community members themselves. This raises an issue about possible paternalism and judgements made by officers about people living in regeneration communities.

Some people saw Active Partners as a useful and flexible tool – 'it can be framework or toolkit at all levels'; the 'benchmarks are relevant to every community situation' – whereas others questioned the relevance of Active Partners in all contexts, for example, to the business sector, to rural areas and to city-centre-based SRB schemes. While we would challenge the view that the benchmarks themselves cannot be applied to different contexts, these views did highlight the need for further guidance about applying Active Partners in different contexts and a listing of additional context-specific indicators.

Format of the materials

Some people commented that *Active Partners* (Yorkshire Forward, 2000) is too big a document and they requested a pared-down version of the benchmarks, produced more as a checklist and ideas for action:

We perhaps need something for communities that is halfway between the full report and the A3 summary. Try to make it look as simple as it is in reality.

The difficulty with moving towards such an approach is that community participation is fairly complex. It is not simple. Many people like the fact that the benchmarks are comprehensive and do not let lead partners off the hook – it would be easy to lose the core principles about participation in a simplified version. The suggestion that gathered most support and addressed both of the above issues was to produce future materials in a clearly referenced, loose-leafed, ring-binder format. This could then be regularly updated with additional materials such as examples of practice.

Good practice incentives

Many people requested good practice case studies and a 'how to do it' manual. The need for an incentive to implement Active Partners was also raised, particularly at the levels where implementation is not a financial criteria. The idea of 'Beacon Schemes' for community participation, where enhanced funding becomes available as a result of good practice in community participation, was suggested by some.

Advice, training, networking and support

There were many requests for more opportunities to share practice and to access training and support to enable partnerships and schemes to effectively apply the Active Partners framework to their own practice. COGS organised 12 sub-regional workshops during the road-testing process and many people seemed to find these useful:

The benchmarks are easy to use if you have been to a workshop and read the booklet.

Suggestions for future support included:

- a mentor available to each partnership

- an 'on tap' consultancy/resource unit

- a single point of contact (telephone line) for all queries

- the availability of a presentation around Active Partners that schemes and community groups could 'call in'

- training opportunities to help people implement the benchmarks (including Yorkshire Forward staff)

- Active Partners courses and training modules for communities and paid workers – leading to professional development qualifications

- local and regional support networks

- dedicated workers within regeneration schemes to facilitate community participation.

Resources

The need for adequate resources for administration and support of community participation was raised many times:

Good community participation takes time and money. This can be problematic where community development is not an implicit part of the SRB bid.

This was borne out by the experience of those actively promoting Active Partners:

We could not have got under way without top slicing our Objective 1 funding; there should be resources available over the 5 per cent administration fee.

The role of Yorkshire Forward

It became clear through the road-testing project that, while Yorkshire Forward had demonstrated a recognised and laudable commitment to the development and implementation of Active Partners, there was a need both to promote and consider the Active Partners benchmarks within the RDA itself and to develop clearer and more consistent assessment procedures to ensure that bad practice is identified, with sanctions if necessary. A number of recommendations related to the RDA were submitted, including the following:

- Yorkshire Forward needs to change its own organisational culture in order to promote community participation.

- Yorkshire Forward should assert its influence – the RDA 'badge' is very useful to highlight the importance of community participation to lead partners that would not otherwise be interested.

- Yorkshire Forward needs to be consistent – it should ensure community participation is monitored in the same way as other outputs.

- Schemes need an honest and empowering recording process (away from tick boxes that seem to encourage dishonesty/untruths).

4 Forward strategy

Beginnings

As has been noted, the emerging findings of the road-testing project were, even before the end of that project, highlighting the usefulness of the benchmarks alongside issues that needed to be addressed in order to support more effective implementation.

Yorkshire Forward itself recognised that, while some of these issues related to practice within the RDA and had to be addressed in house, other issues were more to do with the range of support, training and networking opportunities needed to help communities, schemes and partnerships apply the benchmarks. These could perhaps be provided through commissioned-out services.

The road-testing project itself had provided some level of support for implementation but was a short-term, one-year project. In order to ensure that Active Partners stayed 'live' for the foreseeable future and that implementation could be further improved, embedded and taken into optimum use, Yorkshire Forward committed itself in Autumn 2001 to the development of a clear forward strategy for implementation.

JRF provided funding to resource further research and the development of strategic recommendations in the belief that this would help to put in place the final stage of a theory-to-practice development:

> *This seems a rare opportunity to follow an idea through from theory, through piloting, to mainstream practice.* Active Partners, *and the parallel publication* Auditing Community Participation, *have helped to nail down the formerly woolly intentions of community involvement into some more solid benchmarks and targets. We can now know how this will translate into practice, and be absorbed into mainstream regeneration culture.*
> (Summary of JRF Project Proposal: Active Partners from Pilot to Mainstream, Peter Marcus, 2001)

We, COGS, were again contracted as it was felt that our involvement throughout the developments up to this point put us in the best position to carry out this work.

Developing the strategy

The objective of this strategic work was to carry out an independent assessment of needs, possibilities and issues around the future implementation of Active Partners in order to develop clear and detailed proposals for a forward strategy. It was crucial that any proposed strategy had the support and ownership of the key stakeholders involved. Thus, the approach was to facilitate discussions around emerging options and to work through any conflicting views in order to seek consensus.

The main discussion arena for the work was through Active Partners Reference Group meetings. These were used to develop ideas, to share lessons from elsewhere and to begin to discuss emerging issues and differences. A number of people from outside the region who had particular experience/ expertise were invited to two of these meetings. Discussions focused mainly on three aspects of the Active Partners forward strategy:

1 the key areas of activity that should be included within the strategy

2 the viability of some activities being carried out through a commissioning arrangement

3 alternative management models for commissioned work.

Throughout this process it was important not just to consider how the Active Partners benchmarks themselves could be developed and their implementation supported, but also to begin to explore how the future development of Active Partners could inform and link into related developments in regeneration and Neighbourhood Renewal. This exploration included research into developing audit and assessment strategies, as well as the changing picture of agency roles and Neighbourhood Renewal developments. We carried out desk-top research and follow-up meetings and conversations which helped to begin the mapping of such related developments.

We discovered a wide range of interest and activity in processes for achieving and assessing community participation and its impact. Developments are taking place at both national and regional levels although they are not always well co-ordinated. Through our discussions we began to log related developments drawn from the wider context of regeneration and Neighbourhood Renewal that should be taken into account in the Active Partners forward strategy (see Appendix 4). It was felt that linkages with policy makers and other strategic players would be essential to the successful implementation of Active Partners in all possible arenas. A closer working relationship with the Neighbourhood Renewal Unit nationally and with regional agencies was a logical next step. Discussions were held with representatives from both the Government Office and the Regional Assembly to explore their interest in, and commitment to, the development of Active Partners. In our discussions at regional level, many developments stemming from the Neighbourhood Renewal agenda that could benefit by linking into Active Partners were noted.

Government Office was committed to continued involvement in the future of Active Partners. It recognised Active Partners as a useful framework, relevant and applicable to many of the programmes and partnerships for which it is responsible. For example, officers within Government Office for Yorkshire and the Humber (GOYH) saw Active Partners as a potential tool for:

- monitoring, self-assessment and validation systems for Local Strategic Partnerships and identifying learning needs

- including community participation in the criteria being developed for the performance management system being developed for New Deal for Communities (NDC) and Neighbourhood Management Pathfinders

- use by the proposed Regional Panels of Advisers

- planning engagement strategies in the Community Empowerment Fund networks

- putting together Community Cohesion strategies.

GOYH staff saw Active Partners to have relevance to the regional action plan for the Neighbourhood Renewal Skills and Knowledge Strategy and it was also noted that communities could be supported in their use of the benchmarks via the Community Learning Chests.

The Regional Assembly, which has a strategic and monitoring role in the region, providing regional accountability for Yorkshire Forward, was also committed to ongoing involvement in Active Partners. The Assembly was involved in the teams being established to accredit Local Strategic Partnerships (LSPs) and saw that, following the accreditation process, LSPs could use Active Partners to implement their learning action plans. There was also potential relevance for Active Partners in the Regional Centre of Excellence, once that was established.

Mapping the tasks

Clearly, Active Partners has potential applications, either as it stood or with adaptations, in a number of arenas and at several levels. Indeed, COGS discovered that the benchmarks were already in use, sometimes in unexpected types of projects and structures. At the same time, it was clear that many community regeneration projects funded by SRB were not as well informed as Yorkshire Forward had intended when it first approved the development of Active Partners. Thus, conversant with the findings of the road-testing project and other research, and mindful of the original objective of Active Partners, the Reference Group turned its attention to a forward strategy. It began to map the key areas of work that should be included in this forward strategy and considered which areas of work needed to be undertaken internally by Yorkshire Forward and which might be commissioned out. Underlying this approach was the intention by the Reference Group not to run before it could walk. The potential of Active Partners was (and is) a broad and exciting landscape. It was important to proceed (if somewhat slowly) to create adequate and appropriate means by which this landscape could be developed. The Reference Group therefore concentrated first on the original objective: SRB schemes.

Key aims of a forward strategy were seen to include:

• to ensure that Active Partners is a permanent part of a Yorkshire Forward checklist

• to provide ongoing induction, support and training for Yorkshire Forward partnerships and schemes

• to share and promote best practice

• to carry out an ongoing review and evaluation.

Considering possibilities for commissioning out
Yorkshire Forward had initially suggested the commissioning out of some work around Active Partners. It was 'staff capped' and unable to use more staff time on the project but could commission an external organisation to undertake specific work. There was, for many, an initial concern that Yorkshire Forward could be seen to be distancing itself from the Active Partners work, deferring its responsibilities and minimising any real clout to implementation through any commissioning out arrangement. However, discussion of the overall work programme required

led to an agreement that, while some areas of work could appropriately be commissioned out, key areas of work needed to be addressed by Yorkshire Forward itself and carried forward internally, within and across agency departments.

Following this agreement, the Reference Group considered alternative models for commissioning-out arrangements – through the establishment of a new independent project or through an existing organisation. Discussions about these alternative proposals highlighted a number of factors and concerns to be considered in deciding on the preferred way forward.

• There had to be a status and a level of independence that enabled those involved in the work to say 'hard things to powerful people'.

• It was important that work around Active Partners maintained its own clear identity and profile.

• The work needed to be seen to have the support and clout of all the regional partners who were backing it and not just of the voluntary and community sector.

• Effective development depended on the continued ownership, involvement and influence of both key institutions/agencies and community interests.

• Management structures needed to be kept as simple as possible in order to deliver.

• Any workers employed would need effective management, support and back-up.

The conclusion by the Reference Group was that the most appropriate arrangement for commissioning out would be by funding the Regional Forum for Voluntary and Community Organisations to develop a project, the Active Partners Unit. This Unit would have a clear independent function to develop work around Active Partners. Strategic management responsibilities would be delegated to a dedicated management committee with key stakeholder representation.

Strategic proposals

Based on the research carried out and discussions summarised above, the Active Partners Reference Group and Yorkshire Forward agreed strategic proposals based on four recommendations:

1 that Yorkshire Forward retains and consolidates some of its current responsibility around Active Partners

2 that an Active Partners Unit be established to develop complementary work around Active Partners and its application

3 that there are clear lines of communication and co-ordination of strategy and policy development between Yorkshire Forward and the Active Partners Unit

4 that key stakeholder agencies within the region, and in particular GOYH, be encouraged to adopt Active Partners as a strategic framework for community participation in regeneration/ renewal type programmes.

The strategic proposals were intended as a starting point for the development of the Active Partners Unit in association with Yorkshire Forward. They were reviewed and adapted as the arrangements for the Unit developed.

Respective roles and responsibilities

Yorkshire Forward
It was agreed that Yorkshire Forward should:

• have ownership of Active Partners

• improve its own understanding of community participation and ensure clarity, consistency and rigour in assessment processes, including calling to account those partnerships and schemes that fail to implement sufficiently well informed community participation strategies

• adopt a training and development programme for relevant Yorkshire Forward staff, for example, Inclusion Officers

• raise awareness of, brief Yorkshire Forward representatives on, and integrate Active Partners across all areas of Yorkshire Forward operation including by the production, review and dissemination of the Active Partners resource materials

• implement Active Partners within programme appraisal and assessment procedures by developing a more co-ordinated approach for assessing partnerships and schemes

• initiate a procedure through which community members can call to attention and challenge bad practice in relation to community participation within Yorkshire Forward funded partnerships

• publicise its commitment to community participation

• connect with related developments in the region to share experience of implementing Active Partners and contribute to the development of common approaches to assessing and supporting community participation

• promote Active Partners across other RDAs and nationally, and contribute to related national developments

• assess the impact of community participation on economic and quality of life outcomes

• arrange for the commissioning out of additional activities required to support the development and implementation of Active Partners.

Active Partners Unit
The purpose of the Active Partners Unit was agreed to be:

To promote and support the application of Active Partners as a strategic approach to community participation in regeneration/renewal programmes across the Yorkshire and Humber region.

The aims of the Unit would be to:

- raise awareness of Active Partners and the benchmarks

- develop the Active Partners support materials

- provide consultancy, information and training for the effective use of the Active Partners materials

- gather and disseminate relevant information and provide a 'signposting' service

- promote and contribute to the development of co-ordinated approaches to community participation across the range of regeneration and renewal programmes at regional and national levels

- encourage and enable networking and the sharing of good practice regarding successful strategies for community participation.

The terms of reference of the Unit were developed from these aims.

Accountable body

Yorkshire Forward agreed to commission the Regional Forum to host the Active Partners Unit under contract with review. The overall strategic direction of the Unit was originally conceived as resting with an Active Partners Management Group. At the conclusion of COGS' involvement, discussions were continuing as to the best way for the Active Partners Unit, with its Management Group, to operate. The Active Partners Management Group developed from the Regional Reference Group with representatives from Yorkshire Forward; the Regional Forum; GOYH; Y&H Regional Assembly; the Churches Regional Commission; and interest and community groups

in the region. The Unit itself has a staff establishment of a Head of Unit, a Networking and Training Officer, an Information and Training Officer and an Administrator (see Appendix 5).

The challenges ahead

Frameworks and tools such as Active Partners are often developed in such a way that they are made available only for those who want to use them and are not embedded into procedures and practice. This report describes the more proactive, and challenging, process through which Active Partners has developed from an initial concept to a forward strategy for implementation across the region. Yet, there are many challenges ahead if the benchmarks are to have their intended impact on enhanced community participation.

An increasing number of regeneration partnerships and schemes, both within the Yorkshire and Humber region and beyond, are finding the Active Partners benchmarks a useful framework and tool for strategic thinking. However, others continue to give very token consideration to the crucial but often slow and complex process of effective community participation. There is much work around both the scrutinising and support levels needed to embed fully the elements of practice outlined in Active Partners into the reality of regeneration. This will require those policy makers, accountable bodies, partnerships, schemes and projects involved in regeneration to consider their own practice in relation to community participation. In such an exploration, they must recognise what they are doing well but also identify where they are failing to address and overcome the range of barriers that prevent communities from participating as they would wish.

The other key challenge for the future is to develop a co-ordinated and coherent approach to the community involvement measures (e.g.

University of Ulster LIBRARY

27

References

Burns, Danny and Taylor, Marilyn (2000) *Auditing Community Participation – an Assessment Handbook.* Bristol: Policy Press

COGS (2001a) *Active Partners – Guidance Notes for Partnerships.* Sheffield: COGS in association with the Regional Forum

COGS (2001b) *Active Partners – Benchmarking Community Participation, Guidance Notes for Communities.* Sheffield: COGS in association with the Regional Forum

Yorkshire Forward (2000) *Active Partners – Benchmarking Community Participation in Regeneration.* Leeds: Yorkshire Forward (free report available from Yorkshire Forward, Victoria House, 2 Victoria Place, Leeds LS11 5AE. Tel. 0113 3949600)

Appendix 1

Some of the questions raised from literature review

- Who makes up local communities?

- Do you understand the different interests in the community and their needs? How?

- How is the potential for diverse involvement created?

- How will you ensure those not normally involved are encouraged to do so and what participatory methods will you use to access them?

- What support is available to help you build the appropriate structures and skills required for community involvement?

- What approaches are you adopting to build the above?

- In what way are your participation mechanisms developmental rather than one off?

- How will you feedback to people?

- How else can you illustrate your commitment to community involvement?

- What are the routes to involvement, aside from being on a committee?

- What methods of consultation do you use?

- What training is offered to officers with a consultative role?

- Are you open to feedback/are organisational structures sufficiently flexible?

- Is there a commitment from other departments and agencies?

- What percentage of resources are devoted to participation?

- How is wider community representation supplemented by wider consultation, local delivery agents, etc.?

- How rigorous is the consultation process and timing? What are the costs and resources?

- How is community networking resourced outside the local area as well as within it?

- What do community representatives get out of it? Why should they get involved? How can they use their skills and expertise to move on?

- Who do community representatives really represent? What do they do with information? What mechanisms exist to feed back and consult with their communities? How do they deal with board confidentiality? As a member of the partnership, can they campaign against it?

- How do procedures assist community representatives to undertake their role effectively, e.g. training support workers, access to administration resources?

- Is the representative structure resourced and what are the costs?

- How can community representatives' time be used economically so that it does not detract from other priorities?

- How are volunteers paid or compensated for their investment? Are services and administration available to them? How much does this cost?

- Where are decisions really taken? Who holds the power?

- What are the objectives of participation?

- Is there any commitment to redistribution of power?

- How have communities influenced and shifted the culture of other partners?

- How can local communities maximise their influence?

- Are there mechanisms in place to ensure that those community needs that emerge can be actioned?

- Has the community had any influence in weighting proposals?

- Who are the delivery agents?

- What is the percentage of money delivered through community groups?

- Who controls money? How much money? How much does it cost to administrate?

- Who controls information and is there a strategy? How much is spent on implementing the strategy?

- Are skills and experience 'bought in'? How much does it cost and what has been its value?

- What does the organisation want to achieve from the participation process?

- What are the boundaries of the task? What is fixed and what is still open?

- What level of participation is appropriate with the different outside interests?

- Can the organisation respond to the outcomes of the process or is it intending to manipulate the participants towards predetermined outcomes?

- What is the 'real' agenda? Are there any hidden agendas?

- What is the history of the issues and what are the positions of the various parties?

- Who owns the process within the organisation? Is there more than one owner and, if so, how will this be managed?

- Are the senior officers and politicians prepared to make a public commitment and to be accessible to the participants?

- Who is involved internally? Have they got their internal act together? Are they really committed to the process? Will they stick at it when the going gets tough?

- What resources are available? How much time is there?

- How does this measure up to the support or involvement expected by community interests?

- What are the opportunities for reflection and appraisal?

- How are you widening your membership?

- Have you achieved what you set out to do?

- Is everyone happy with the level of involvement?

- What are the lessons?

- Costing of resources: have all resources been costed and valued, e.g. work equity by community groups?

- What about a gender and race audit of regeneration policies?

- Learning from partners: is this measured and appraised?

- Has the community engaged in oppositional tactics?

- Is there planning for the long-term sustainability of the partnership at the start?

- Does the whole partnership share a vision – has this ever been explored?

Appendix 2

Emerging themes from the development workshops

Community empowerment dimensions

Personal learning and development

- Recognising and valuing skills, confidence and knowledge that people already have.

- Supportive environment.

- Developing self-confidence and self-esteem.

- A belief in the infinite capacities of everyone.

- Starting where a person is at, not at the level of someone else's perception.

- Better employment opportunities for *all*. Projects should recognise the skills and experiences in the community and employ them instead of expecting everything for nothing.

- Identifying the needs perceived by local people.

- Confidence and support, e.g. workshops to give people more confidence to be involved.

- Being able to do it together – not just for certain levels of experience.

- Relevance – community-led agenda for training. Training needs should emerge from activity – not be offered prior to decisions about/around priorities.

- Recognition that learning can be fun and does not have to lead to credits.

- Look at ability within community to devise and deliver training.

- Communities teaching the professionals – 'upside-down' capacity building.

- Recognise quality *not* quantity is important – people are people *not* outputs!

- Learning from others' experiences – case studies of how decisions are *really* made.

- Mentoring/shadowing into public meetings, town hall, partnership meetings, etc.

- Increasing confidence in local people's belief in their ability to make a difference.

- More opportunities for community action through arts and environmental projects.

- Funders (SRB) need to work with communities/ groups on bids building confidence/capacity – not done by dropping people in at the deep end.

- Learning to involve people in a non-bureaucratic way.

Equality

- Respect for difference.

- Decision makers' meet people on their own ground.

- Old and young need to be in contact with each other.

- Children and young people need to be valued.

- More attention to people facing multiple discrimination.

- Value the contribution of unpaid workers too.

- Identify those without a voice.

- Everyone's views represented.

- Better communication – getting the message across.

- Translate into community languages.

- Language – jargon barrier.

- Can everyone gain access to facilities?

- Awareness of why people do not get involved?

- Consider seriously the effects of poverty as a barrier.

- Ensure that paid people do not see themselves (even unconsciously) as more equal than unpaid activists. 'Professionals' are often people who live there – not the 'officials'.

- Get rid of bidding mechanism. Look at new ways of distributing regeneration funds – co-operation replacing competition.

- Community identity from the bottom up.

- The money should be held by local communities who know, not the local authorities who *think* they know.

- Striving to create a more level playing field from which to start.

- Have courage to embrace *broad* definitions of outputs and outcomes.

- Access to resources for the community.

- Government guidelines should recognise the diversity of communities and be more flexible.

- Tackle root causes of inequality.

- Equal opportunities policies needed.

- Don't just listen to those with the loudest voices.

Organisation
- Recognition and acceptance of overlapping agendas – co-operation instead of competition.

- Partnership building to deliver a better service between organisations.

- The need for joint ventures across communities and the need to develop an agenda/strategy for the community sector.

- Networking.

- Some means of obtaining a bigger and broader vision.

- Minority ethnic community organisations have support to link with other community-based organisations.

- Peer support and mentoring between projects.

- Need greater communication and sharing of information.

- Local starting points not created from the outside.

- Early help from community development workers – to bring together and to help constitute sustainable groups.

- Openness and mutual listening between different groups.

- Simplifying some funding applications.

- The community sector should be resourced at the same level as others in terms of administration/research, etc. to enable organisation for equal participation.

- Being allowed to deliver and given the resources to do so.

- Induction and support to operate in partnership organisations.

- Expenses paid on time or up front.

- More information so that people feel more informed and confident to have their say.

- Community organisations identify their own needs, and are allowed to develop at their own pace and in their own chosen direction.

- Training for volunteer committees to strengthen management skills.

- Sustainability – what happens when the agenda moves on from participation to 'hard' economics?

- The right language(s) including Braille, plain English, sign language.

- Capacity to deal with conflict.

- Need for more creative community group activity.

Influence

- Believing it might be possible to *have* some influence.

- Don't just pay lip service to 'community' or use us to gain credibility.

- The decision makers to listen and act on what the community says – not the other way round.

- Communities in at the beginning of strategic planning and development, etc.

- Having the money – being the purchasers.

- Full participation – control of decision making.

- Respect from statutory agencies, their employees and elected representatives.

- Recognition that participation and influence takes *time* to happen well.

- Start local and work up – not vice versa.

- Access to information and knowledge.

- Knowledge of the rules.

- Impartial support so people understand decision-making processes and the impacts of particular decisions.

- Don't just listen to one or two 'leaders'. A few unaccountable leaders do not make participation.

- Meeting in neutral or non-threatening environment.

- Clarity of structures and processes you are trying to engage with – need structures that enable the least confident to have their say.

- Infiltration at all levels, involvement in decisions at all levels.

- Accessibility of decision makers.

- Transparent procedures and processes for all partners.

- Having a community vision – community plans for the whole community.

- Mentoring – linking workers with community members.

- Resources to enable communities to have impact.

- A 'secretariat' for communities.

Pre-bid stage objectives

1 To involve local people and local communities in the identification, evidencing and interpretation of community needs.

2 To incorporate the ideas of local people in bids/ delivery plans:
   - resourcing the working up of local ideas
   - including ideas from marginalised communities
   - raising awareness of bid planning/ preparation.

3 To ensure that local people understand language, process and information:
   - bidding guidance should be produced in an accessible form
   - clear process for developing bids
   - major bodies to recognise and communicate the importance of local input so that people feel confident they can make a difference.

4 To build a strong community body to co-ordinate the regeneration programme:
   - ensuring inclusive involvement and meaningful representation at all levels
   - providing effective models/guidelines for the development of an involvement strategy.

Scheme-level objectives

1 To enable local people to play a role in all decision making:
   - setting targets for numbers of people involved/consulted

- ensuring local people have a balance of power on management boards
- measurement of the nature of local involvement
- identifying barriers to different people's involvement and taking steps to overcome these
- measurement of satisfaction levels of extent to which projects meet needs
- employment of local people as development workers.

2 To ensure that all partnership-level groups demonstrate equality, diversity, power sharing, openness and respect:
- increasing community knowledge of issues, structures, meetings and how to feed into partnership level.

3 To improve the skills needed to participate at scheme level:
- providing training and induction for community representatives.

Project-level objectives

1 To allow some flexibility and minimise bureaucracy:
- simplification of forms and communication ('dejargonise')
- providing funding for pre-project bid activities, e.g. research.

2 To communicate and feed back to the wider community using a range of methods:
- ensuring that key project workers are based locally and are accessible to community members.

Wider community outreach

1 To involve the community in a positive way:
- measurement of number of people involved and diversity of participants
- developing qualitative measures of involvement

- ensuring proactive encouragement of involvement is a continuous process.

2 To equalise power relationships regarding information:
- ensuring equal access to appropriate information
- balancing top-down/bottom-up flow of information
- developing contact with people really at the grass-roots
- targeting marginalised groups.

3 To develop a co-ordinated information strategy:
- sharing resources for information
- developing a database of all local groups
- supporting community networking
- developing a listing of useful resources and contacts.

4 To develop soft and more relevant outputs set by local community groups:
- qualitative participation outputs
- flexible timescales.

Key processes

- Networking – sharing what has and what has not worked.
- Participatory research.
- Respect and acknowledgement.
- Access for all.
- Dedicated officers and secretariat support.
- Mentoring.
- Different approaches for different people.
- Skills and awareness training for lead partners and external agencies.

Resources

- Community information workers.
- Community development workers.

- Yorkshire Forward resourcing of information/ training regarding regeneration processes and structures.

- Community bases – desks, IT, photocopiers, telephones.

- More money.

Appendix 3

Active Partners benchmarks with key considerations

Benchmarks	Key considerations
Influence	
The community is recognised and valued as an equal partner at all stages of the process.	Who has had the first word in your regeneration strategy and how are community agendas reflected from day one and throughout the process? How are community members made to feel valued as equal partners?
There is meaningful community representation on all decision-making bodies from initiation.	How are communities represented on decision-making groups (in addition to/instead of the bigger players such as local councillors)? How are your decision-making processes enabling communities to be heard and to influence?
All community members have the opportunity to participate.	How are you supporting community networks/structures through which all communities can contribute to decision making? What are the range of opportunities, e.g. creative/flexible approaches, through which community members can influence decisions?
Communities have access to and control over resources.	In what ways do regeneration workers and decision makers make themselves accessible to community members? How is community control of resources being increased?
Evaluation of regeneration partnerships incorporates a community agenda.	How are you ensuring community ownership of evaluation processes?
Inclusivity	
The diversity of local communities and interests are reflected at all levels of the regeneration process.	What steps are you taking to ensure that all communities can be involved with and influence regeneration strategy and activity? What actions are you taking to ensure that representation by all partner agencies and staff composition reflect the gender balance and ethnic diversity of the geographical area?
Equal opportunities policies are in place and implemented.	What support and training is offered to the development of equal opportunities policies and anti-discriminatory practice? How are you monitoring and reviewing practice in relation to equal opportunities?
Unpaid workers/volunteer activists are valued.	How do you support and resource unpaid workers and voluntary activists? What opportunities do you provide for their personal development and career progression?

(Continued overleaf)

Benchmarks	Key considerations	*(continued)*
Communication A two-way information strategy is developed and implemented.	How do you ensure that information is clear and accessible and reaches all communities in time for it to be acted on? How are those involved in regeneration informed about the communities with whom they are working?	
Programme and project procedures are clear and accessible.	What steps are you taking to ensure that scheme procedures facilitate community participation rather than act as a barrier?	
Capacity Communities are resourced to participate.	What resources are provided for the development of community-led networks and community groups? What support is provided for community members and community representatives? What strategy is in place to support community-led sustainability?	
Understanding, knowledge and skills are developed to support partnership working.	How are you ensuring that all partners (including senior people from the public and private sectors) develop the understanding, knowledge and skills to work in partnership and engage with communities? What training is provided and who is participating in both the delivery and learning?	

Appendix 4

Potential linkages with Active Partners work

Project	Potential linkage
Neighbourhood Renewal (Department of the Environment, Transport and the Regions [DETR])	
Accreditation of Local Strategic Partnerships	GOYH currently assessing LSPs. Six criteria with strong emphasis on community inclusion and participation. Requirement for ongoing assessment and development against agreed Action Plan (D).
Community Empowerment Fund	Lead Bodies identified (GOYH/Regional Forum) at district level; Community Chests being set up. *Resources available to support community participation in LSPs (D).*
Performance Management System	Being developed by Neighbourhood Renewal Unit (NRU) for New Deal for Communities (NDC) and Neighbourhood Management. *Approx. 20 criteria – community development/participation not covered (P).*
Neighbourhood Renewal Advisers	Being recruited by NRU to provide expert advice on regeneration to neighbourhood partnerships.
Skills and Knowledge Strategy	Under development by NRU. Includes: National study commissioned on skills and competencies required for Neighbourhood Renewal. Residents' Consultancies being piloted (NRU/Department for Education and Skills [DfES]). Pilot proposals being invited on innovative approaches to deliver Neighbourhood Renewal (NR) skills and knowledge.
Regional Skills and Knowledge strategy	Regional Action Plan being drawn up by GOYH to deliver national strategy. *Some resources may be available to deliver strategy, including training for GOYH staff (D).*
Regional Panel of Advisers	To support communities in NR areas; will complement national advisers programme.
Community Learning Chests	Small grants to support learning opportunities for individuals/partnerships. Administered alongside NR Community Chests.
Regional Centres of Excellence	To deliver neighbourhood renewal skills to professionals and practitioners. Yorkshire and the Humber being considered for a 'part-virtual' centre. Taken forward by RDA + Regional Assembly with input from GOYH. *Potential future home for Active Partners Unit (APU) (P).*
Audit Commission	
Mainstreaming anti-poverty initiatives	Project to improve mainstreaming of urban regeneration pilots by bending mainstream services, changing culture and attitudes, changing what mainstream services do.
Quality of Life indicators	Indicators on Community Development and Social Capital being developed as part of Best Value Review.

(Continued overleaf)

Project	Potential linkage	*(Continued)*
Regional Co-ordination Unit (Cabinet Office)		
Area Based Initiatives Forum	Improve links and communication around Area Based Initiatives (ABIs); help create a body of best practice through electronic network and regular meetings. Topics will include Partnership Best Practice.	
Active Communities Unit (Home Office)		
Measuring community strength	Developing indicators to be rolled out across government departments.	
Countryside Agency		
Market Towns Initiative Healthcheck	A tool to help local people prepare an action plan to revitalise their town. Yorkshire Forward/Countryside Agency promoting the use of Active Partners in assessment and monitoring of Action Plans (D).	
Vital Villages	Local communities being asked to produce Parish Plans (D). Vital Villages (VV) officers being recruited by Countryside Agency and rural Community Council.	
Investors in Communities (DETR, Housing Corporation, JRF)	Pilot development of accreditation standards for housing associations and local communities for developing their abilities and skills to tackle local problems. Based on Investors in People model.	
Local Councils Association		
Quality Councils	Empower parish councils and develop rural leadership.	
National Network of Regeneration Partnerships	NRU funding a national appointment to facilitate regional regeneration networks. Existing models: Regeneration Exchange NE; Regeneration Network NW. *Structures and funding to be agreed at regional level (P).*	
South Yorkshire Objective 1 programme		
Priority 4	Measure 22: Academy of Community Leaders linking with NRU, Northern College, etc. Building and accrediting skills for community activists.	
North Yorkshire County Council (NYCC)		
Community Investment Prospectus	Required from 34 communities by NYCC SRB 'Developing Futures' bid. Community Link officers recruited. Includes AP benchmarking requirements (D).	

Note: P = Policy D = Delivery.

Appendix 5

Outline Active Partners Unit job profiles

Head of Unit

Job profile

Areas of responsibility will include the following:

- To co-ordinate and lead the work programme of the Unit.

- To provide line management to the Active Partners Unit staff team.

- To promote the work of the Unit and develop strategic and practice links with other agencies and partnerships.

- To represent the Active Partners Unit, where appropriate, at regional and national level.

- To service and co-ordinate meetings of the Management Group.

- To assist the Development Officers in the development and provision of training and consultancy support to regeneration partnerships and schemes.

Person profile

The following skills and understanding will be required:

- Knowledge and understanding of current developments related to neighbourhood renewal and regeneration.

- Experience of working at a policy and strategic level.

- Experience of working with partnerships and communities.

- Understanding of community development, community participation and barriers to engagement.

- Excellent interpersonal, influencing, oral and communication skills.

- Experience of managing people and projects.

- Experience and skills in training and facilitation.

- Understanding of equal opportunities and anti-discriminatory practice.

Active Partners Networking and Training Officer

Job profile

Areas of responsibility will include the following:

- To develop and deliver Active Partners training programmes for partnerships and schemes, community members and Yorkshire Forward staff.

- To provide consultancy support to partnerships and schemes.

- To promote and raise awareness of Active Partners through community groups and networks.

- To organise regular networking events for both partnerships/schemes and community members.

- To facilitate other forms of networking around community participation.

- To provide a basic advice service through telephone, email and surgeries.

Person profile

The following skills and understanding will be required:

- Experience of working with partnerships and communities at neighbourhood level.

- Experience and understanding of community development, community participation and barriers to engagement.

- Experience and understanding in developing and delivering training.

- Excellent facilitation, interpersonal and communication skills.

- Skills and experience in organising training courses and events.

- Understanding and skills in networking.

- Understanding of equal opportunities and anti-discriminatory practice.

Active Partners Information and Training Officer

Job profile
Areas of responsibility will include the following:

- To develop and deliver Active Partners training programmes for partnerships and schemes, community members and Yorkshire Forward staff.

- To provide consultancy support to partnerships and schemes.

- To provide a basic advice service through telephone, email and surgeries.

- To co-ordinate the writing and production of promotional and resource materials.

- To gather, collate and store examples of practice and development.

Person profile
The following skills and understanding will be required:

- Experience of working with partnerships and communities at neighbourhood level.

- Experience and understanding of community development, community participation and barriers to engagement.

- Experience and understanding in developing and delivering training.

- Excellent facilitation, interpersonal and communication skills.

- Skills and experience in organising training courses and events.

- Experience and skills in writing, editing and design of resource materials.

- Understanding of equal opportunities and anti-discriminatory practice.

- Awareness of the use of different media to meet diverse communication needs, e.g. translation into community languages, large print, audio tapes, etc.

Administrator (part-time, 28 hours per week)

Job profile
Areas of responsibility will include the following:

- To set up and maintain paper- and computer-based information systems.

- To maintain any website, email groups, etc. established by the unit.

- To respond to general enquiries.

- To manage the Active Partners Unit office(s).

- To administer training course, events, conferences, etc. organised through the Unit.

- To prepare and monitor project budgets.

Person profile
The following skills and understanding will be required:

- Computer literacy in word processing, layout, spreadsheets and databases.

- Excellent administrative and organisational skills.

- Understanding of administrative systems.

- Knowledge and experience of bookkeeping and preparing budgets.

benchmarking, performance management, best value, etc.) being implemented across an increasing range of programmes and initiatives related to regeneration that are often impacting on the same communities. While a key purpose of Active Partners is to provide a framework against which regeneration partnerships and schemes should be accountable both to their funding bodies and their communities, enthusiasm for such a responsibility will dissipate if different and sometimes conflicting requirements are being imposed by other but overlapping programmes. This is not to suggest that everyone should adopt Active Partners. However, what the story described here demonstrates is that Active Partners can make a valid and valuable contribution to such a long-term development.

Appendix 6

Resources and contacts

Active Partners – Benchmarking Community Participation in Regeneration
Yorkshire Forward (2000)
Includes the benchmarking framework and guidelines, including key considerations and suggested indicators and good practice for each benchmark
Free report available from:
Yorkshire Forward
Victoria House
2 Victoria Place
Leeds LS11 5AE
Tel. 0113 3949600

Active Partners Unit
C/o Yorkshire and the Humber Regional Forum for Voluntary and Community Organisations
2nd Floor, Goodbard House
15 Infirmary Street
Leeds LS1 2JS
Tel. 0113 2001390
Email office@activepartners.org.uk

COGS
235A London Road
Sheffield S2 4NF
Tel./fax 0114 2554747
Email mail@cogs.solis.co.uk

Auditing Community Participation – an Assessment Handbook
By Danny Burns and Marilyn Taylor (2000)
ISBN 1 86134 271 3
£13.95
Available from:
The Policy Press
34 Tyndall's Park Road
Bristol BS8 1PY
Tel. 0117 9546800
or Joseph Rowntree Foundation
www.jrf.org.uk